Tasty and Exotic Foods

Tempt your taste buds with these tasty and exotic foods of the tropics.

Claudia Foleng-Achunche

PUBLISH AMERICA

PublishAmerica
Baltimore

First printing

ISBN: 1-4137-5096-6
PUBLISHED BY PUBLISHAMERICA, LLLP
www.publishamerica.com
Baltimore

Printed in the United States of America

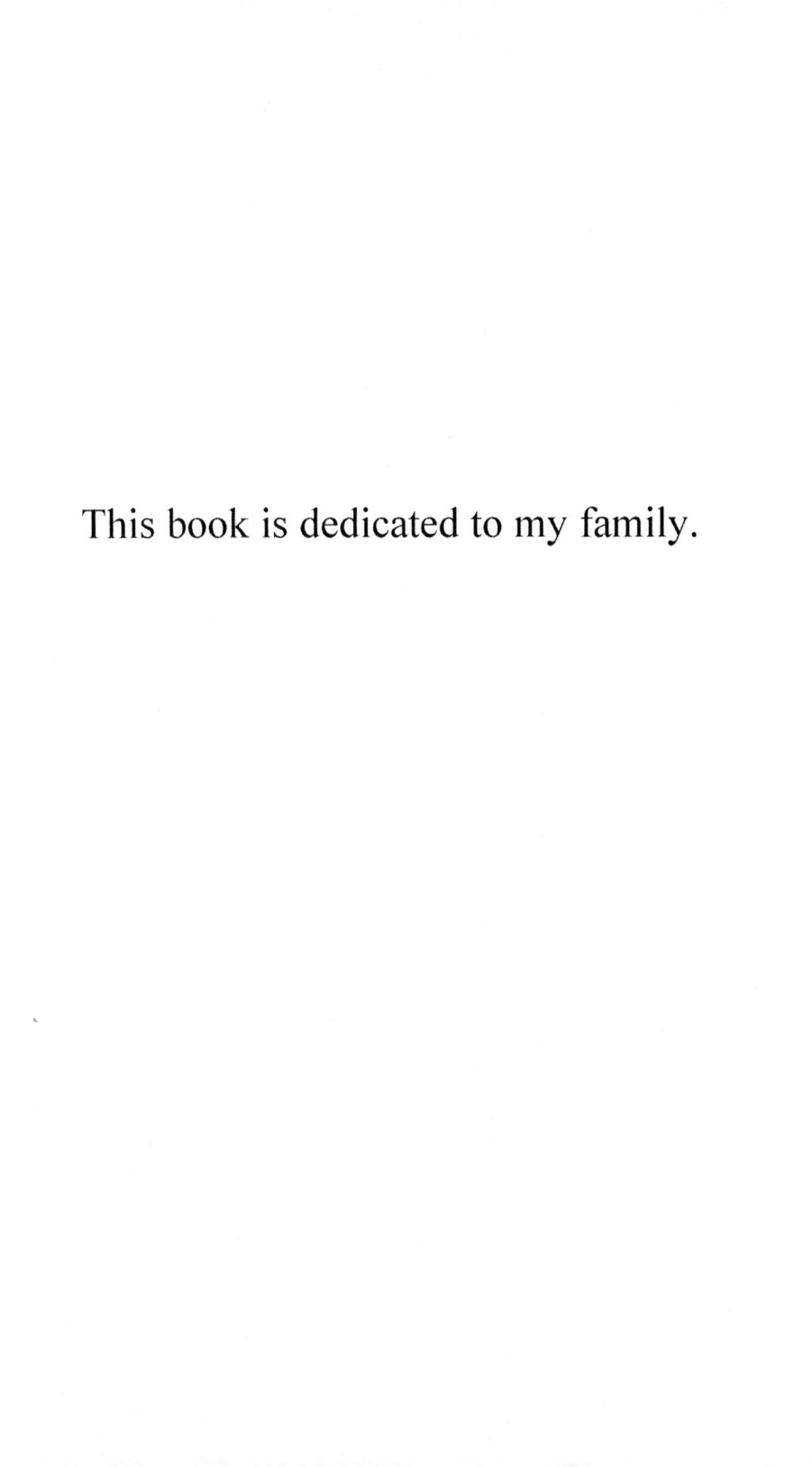

This book is dedicated to my family.

Acknowledgments

In God's love I stand and give thanks for his favour and blessings on my life.

In accomplishing this work, there are quite a few people I would like to thank who were vital from its infancy through to completion.

First of all, my thanks go to my Web Design Trainer—Sarah Barnard of www.computerfuture.net. It was through training that I decided to share these delights not just through a website, but also as a book. Thanks for your tireless help.

My family here in England, my blessings and my angels (my beautiful children), Hannah and Harrison, their dad, Eddie, and my sister, Simone, who have supported me a great deal, while I have had to spend most of my time at home getting my work finished. You have been my rock and strength.

My family in Cameroon—my dad, my mum, and my aunty Cecilia, thank you for your care and support in my life, for always being there for me, and especially for your unconditional love.

Thanks to my sisters and brothers, my cousins, and all my aunts and uncles in Cameroon and around the world.

Oh, Judith, during your short life here on earth, you blessed me a great deal. You were loyal, kind, my best friend, and my sister. Thank you for the time we spent together. I miss you so much but I know you are in heaven now in God's Love. And thank you for the beautiful child, Venita, whom you left with us. Thank you all for the love and kindness you've shown me through the years and especially your prayers.

To my grandparents, all my family members, and friends who are also at peace in heaven, thank you for your lives on earth and for your prayers.

Thank you Jude, Marinus, Aunty Ndia Therese, Ndia Joe, Aunty Nicole, Denis, Norbert, and Sister Maureen for your advice and direction through the years. And thank you Bih for your support.

I also wish to thank my friends, especially Julie and Rodney, Dorothy, Debbie, Ndia Bih, Elaine, Julian and Avantika for your support throughout the years, and all my well-wishers. Thank you BK and Bila for your prayers. Thank you Yvonne, Takow, and Ernest for all your help.

To my three godchildren—Harriet, Mumsi, and Karl, thank you for being blessings in my life.

Thank you Ms. Helen Ndofor for your encouragement and wise words.

Thank you Mr. Mbame for the contacts and for helping me promote this book.

Finally, I wish to thank my fans. You've encouraged me to make my passion for good food a reality for the world to enjoy.

Thank you all for your prayers and endless support.

Introduction

In this book, you'll discover the delights of the West African region and its exotic range of foods.

West Africa covers a vast area of Africa, stretching 3,000 km from north to south and 6,000 km from east to west, Cameroon being one of the countries boasts of hundreds of dishes.

Each of the West African countries has made an indigenous mark on the different crops of the region, truly contributing to a blend of cuisine.

The delicious flavours of our sun-blessed region are reflected by the hot sauces to the scrumptiousness of our fruits.

The different dishes range from the fresh and unique root vegetables such as cassava, yams, and cocoyams to our spicy peppers, njangsang, and egusi, with that truly tropical taste and flavour.

The fruits range from the juicy and succulent pawpaw, sunset fleshed mangoes, honey sweet pineapples, smooth and yummy bananas, luscious passion fruits, to tender and fresh coconuts, just to name a few.

This cooking is fresh, homemade, and mouth-watering.

MAKE YOURSELF AT HOME!

Claudia Foleng-Achunche

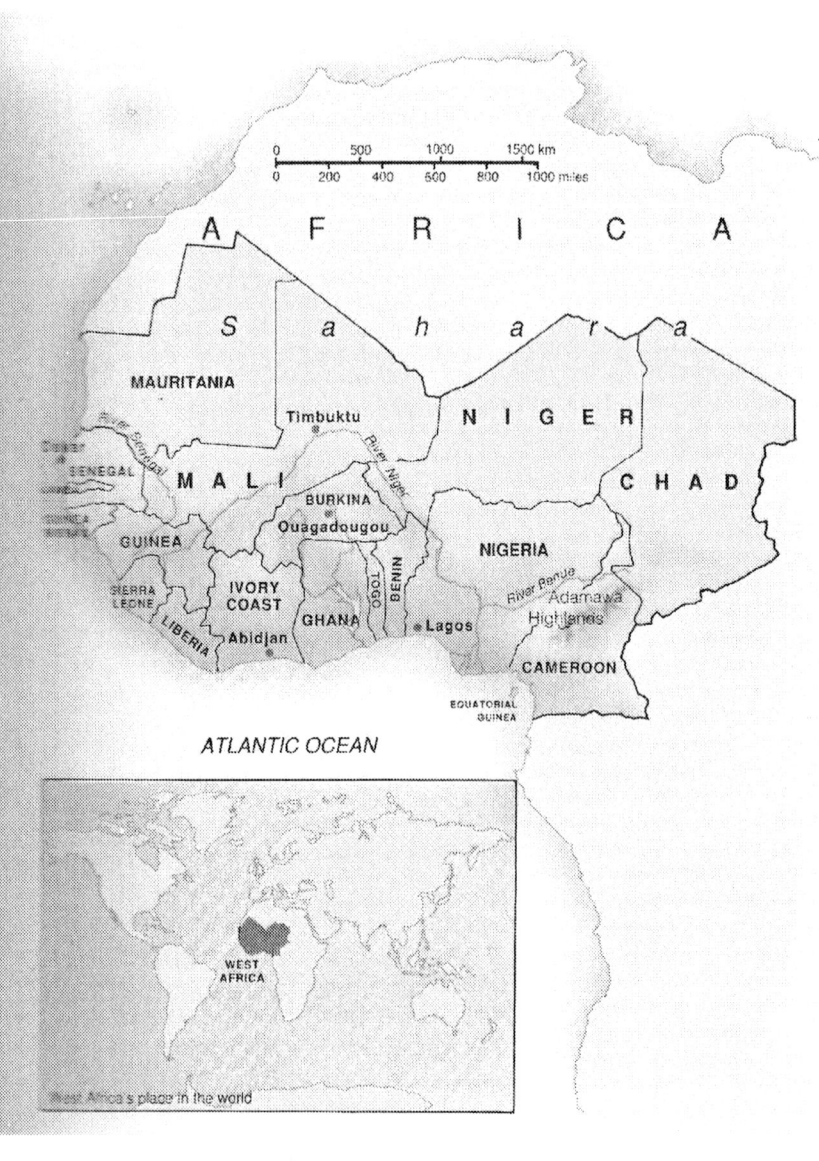

Table of Contents:

Conversion Tables of Measurements

Oven Temperatures:

250°F = 120°C
300°F = 150°C
350°F = 180°C
400°F = 200°C
450°F = 230°C
500°F = 260°C

Volumes:

1 tsp (teaspoon) = 5 ml
1 tbs (tablespoon) = 15 ml
150 ml = ¼ pint
250 ml = ½ pint
500 ml = 1 pint

Weights:

1 ounce = 30 g (grams)
8 ounce = ½ pound
16 ounce = 1 pound
32 ounce = 2 pounds
250 g (grams) = ¼ kilogram
500 g (grams) = ½ kilogram
1000 g (grams) = 1 kilogram

Recipes

Starters

Tasty Vegetable Soup

Ingredients:

1 large onion
3 tbs of cooking oil (olive/vegetable)
100 g frozen mixed vegetables
2 leeks
2 medium sized potatoes
2 tbs of flour
2 Maggi or vegetable Knorr cubes
2 tbs of black pepper
salt to taste

Method:

❖ Peel and wash potatoes.
❖ Chop onion and leeks.
❖ Parboil potatoes, then add leeks and mixed vegetables and simmer.
❖ When cooked, blend together with ½ litre water.
❖ Heat oil in a saucepan, and add chopped onion and flour; stir until golden brown.
❖ Add the blended vegetables, black pepper, and cubes and simmer for 2 minutes.
❖ Remove and strain through a sieve.
❖ Soup should be light enough for drinking.
❖ Garnish with parsley and serve hot.

Serves 4

Fish Pepper Soup

Ingredients:

5 slices of cleaned fresh mackerel fish or any preferred tropical
fish
1 medium sized onion
1 tbs of coarse black pepper
1 tbs of white pepper
100 g of ground njangsang (optional) *See* **glossary**
3 cloves of garlic
2 Maggi cubes
salt to taste

Method:

❖ Wash slices of fish.
❖ Slice onions and grate garlic.
❖ Pour 1 litre of water into a saucepan.
❖ Add ground njangsang, grated garlic, onions, and pepper
(white and black).
❖ Add Maggi cubes or fish seasoning (Dunn River).
❖ Boil for 10 minutes.
❖ Add fish and simmer for 7 minutes.
❖ Serve hot.

Serves 5

Mushroom Pepper Soup

The same as Fish Pepper Soup, except the main ingredient is mushroom and not fish.

Fresh hot chilli peppers can be used as an alternative to black/ white pepper if preferred (see *Glossary*).

Banana & Tomato Salad

Ingredients:

2 fresh medium sized tomatoes
2 ripe bananas
1 tbs chopped onion
1 small lemon
2 tbs of sunflower oil
1 tsp sugar

Method:

❖ Wash and dry tomatoes, banana, and lemon.
❖ Slice tomatoes and arrange in a circle on a plate.
❖ Peel and slice bananas, and place on tomatoes on the plate.
❖ Sprinkle with part of the juice from the lemon and garnish with chopped onions.
❖ Mix oil, remaining lemon juice, and sugar in a separate bowl until well blended.
❖ Pour carefully over the plate and serve **immediately**.

Serves 4

Avocado Paste with Spicy Shrimp, Served with Plantains

Ingredients:

½ lb shrimp, peeled and washed
½ tsp chilli powder
2 cloves garlic (minced)
½ tbs fresh lime juice
½ tsp grated nutmeg
½ tsp cinnamon
½ tsp all purpose seasoning (Dunn River)
3 ripe plantains
salt to taste

For Avocado Paste:

½ avocado (mashed)
½ tbs lime juice
1 clove garlic (minced)
¼ small onion (minced)
salt and ground black pepper

Method:

To make shrimp:

❖ Marinate shrimp with all purpose seasoning and salt; cover and refrigerate for 20 minutes.
❖ Add all the dried seasoning to the shrimp with garlic and lime juice.

❖ Mix together and add salt and black pepper to taste.
❖ Preheat oven and place shrimp in a shallow glass baking dish, lightly greased with olive oil.
❖ Bake for 3 minutes per side or until golden and slightly curled.

To make avocado paste:

❖ Mix all ingredients together, acquiring a puree form.

To make plantains:

❖ Peel ripe plantains and slice or mash (2-inch thick slices or ½ inch thick mashed)
❖ Heat oil in a frying pan and fry sliced pieces on either side until lightly browned and drain out the oil.

Serving:

❖ Place plantains on a serving tray, spread avocado paste on top, and finally place shrimp.
❖ Serve warm.

Serves 6

Meat Suya

Ingredients:

500 g lean beef/pork (boneless)
2 Maggi cubes
1 tsp ground coriander
1 tbs sunflower oil
2 cloves garlic (minced)
8 wooden/metal skewers
1 tsp chilli powder (optional)
1 tsp all purpose seasoning
salt to taste

Method:

❖ Slice meat into ½ inch by 3 inch strips.
❖ Marinate with Maggi cubes, finely chopped onion, chilli powder, coriander, all purpose seasoning, garlic, and salt to taste.
❖ Leave for one hour in a refrigerator.
❖ Thread the meat onto the skewers and varnish with sunflower oil.
❖ Grill for 7 minutes on each side.
❖ Serve hot on its own.

Serves 4

Can also be grilled without the use of skewers.
Chicken can also be used in place of meat for this recipe.

Sweet Potato Starters

Ingredients:

2 medium sized sweet potatoes
vegetable oil for frying
salt to taste
chilli powder (optional)

Method:

- ❖ Simply peel the vegetable and slice into papery thin slices.
- ❖ Fry each vegetable separately in hot oil and drain.
- ❖ Sprinkle with salt and serve as a starter or snack.
- ❖ Serve hot.

Serves 4

For this recipe you can also use yams or cassava.

Grilled Diced Chicken with Chilli Pineapple Dip

Ingredients:

2 lb cubes of chicken (bite size or diced)
1 tbs coriander (ground)
1 tsp turmeric
1 tbs puree fresh garlic
1 tbs vegetable oil
1 tsp salt
2 crushed Maggi cubes

For Chilli Pineapple Dip:

50 g low fat mayonnaise
2 cloves garlic (minced)
50 g chopped fresh pineapple
2 tsp chilli powder
80 ml fresh lime juice
½ chopped small onion
a pinch of salt
a pinch of chopped parsley

Method:

Grilled chicken bites:

❖ Blend all ingredients in a food blender until smooth
❖ Pour over Chicken pieces and marinate for 30 minutes

❖ Grill Marinated chicken in an oven tray for 5 minutes on either side.

Chilli pineapple dip:

❖ Whisk together all ingredients with a fork
❖ Then, sprinkle with chopped parsley
❖ Serve with chicken bites.

Yam Fritters

Ingredients:

1 lb yams (uncooked), peeled, washed, and cut into small pieces
3 garlic cloves
¾ chopped chilli pepper
1 onion (chopped)
1 tbs corn flour
25 g chopped chives
vegetable oil for frying
1 tbs all purpose seasoning (Dunn River)

Method:

❖ Blend all ingredients including the yam pieces, in a food blender to a fine paste, but not watery.
❖ Season well with salt and all purpose seasoning
❖ Drop by tablespoonfuls into hot oil and fry until golden
❖ Serve with **Chilli Pineapple Dip** or **Chilli Mango Dip**.

Chilli Mango Dip

Ingredients:

50 g low fat mayonnaise
2 cloves garlic (minced)
50 g chopped fresh mango
2 tsp chilli powder
80 ml fresh lime juice
½ chopped small onion
a pinch of salt
a pinch of chopped parsley

Method:

- ❖ Whisk together all ingredients with a fork.
- ❖ Then, sprinkle with chopped parsley.
- ❖ Serve with **Chicken Bites** or **Yam Fritters**.

Dodo with Spicy Prawn Tomato Sauce

Ingredients:

2 lb Large peeled prawns
1 tbs all purpose seasoning
2 tsp chilli sauce
½ tsp grated nutmeg
3 cloves minced garlic
1 tsp fresh lime juice
1 can chopped tomatoes or 3 fresh tomatoes
150 g mixed vegetables (chopped carrots, peas, green beans, and sweet corn)
salt to taste

Method:

❖ Marinate prawns with all ingredients except tomatoes and onion, and grill.
❖ Fry onion until golden brown, and add tomatoes, stirring frequently for 7 minutes.
❖ Add grilled prawns, with the stock from marinating, and stir-fry for 3 minutes.
❖ Add mixed vegetables and simmer for 5 minutes.
❖ Serve with **Dodo** (fried plantain chips) See *Core Dishes* for **Dodo**.

Meat Dishes

Groundnut Sauce with Beef

Ingredients:

400 g roasted groundnut or peanut butter
500 g fresh meat (sliced into small pieces)
1 tsp each freshly ground ginger and garlic
1 can chopped tomatoes
1 medium onion
3 tbs groundnut oil
1/8 tsp turmeric
3 Maggi cubes
salt and fresh chilli to taste.

Method:

❖ Boil meat pieces with salt, some slices of onion, and 1 Maggi cube.
❖ Heat oil in a saucepan and add the rest of onion, and stir until golden brown.
❖ Add boiled meat slices and stir for 3 minutes.
❖ Add tomatoes, garlic, and ginger.
❖ Cook sauce on very low heat until there is very little of the sour taste from tomatoes left.
❖ Crush groundnut in dry food processor and set aside, then add ¾ litre water to groundnut paste and mix well until smooth. Add to saucepan.
❖ Add Maggi cubes, salt, and chilli to taste.
❖ Simmer for 10 minutes.
❖ Serve hot with rice or **Boiled Ripe Plantains.**

Serves 6

Chicken or pork can also be used in place of beef for this recipe.

West African Chicken Curry

Ingredients:

500 g chopped chicken
2 medium onions
2 cloves garlic
2 tbs sunflower oil
125 g curry powder
1 tsp puree ginger
2 tsp tomato puree
250 ml warm water
salt and pepper to taste

Method:

❖ Peel and slice onion and garlic finely.
❖ Fry onions and garlic in heated oil in a saucepan.
❖ Add washed and drained chicken pieces and stir constantly until chicken is cooked and golden brown.
❖ Add curry powder and ginger and stir for 2 minutes.
❖ Mix warm water with tomato puree and pour in the saucepan.
❖ Add salt and white pepper or chillies to taste.
❖ Turn into a casserole dish and cover with lid or foil.
❖ Cook for 15 minutes at gas mark 3 (160°C or 325°F)
❖ Serve on a bed of cooked rice or with **Boiled Yams, Plantains** or **Cassava** (see *Core Dishes*).

Jollof Rice

Ingredients:

300 g rice
1 kg lamb slices
1 can chopped tomatoes
250 g mixed vegetable (carrots, peas, sweet corn, peppers)
3 tbs vegetable oil
1 medium onion
2 tbs each mixed seasoning and herbs
(all purpose seasoning, turmeric, basil and thyme)
2 Maggi cubes
2 tbs chilli sauce (optional)
1½ litres water
parsley to garnish

Method:

❖ Boil meat slices with onion, salt, and 1 Maggi cube until tender.
❖ Heat oil in a saucepan and add chopped onions and tomatoes.
❖ Add salt, Maggi cube, mixed seasoning, herbs, and boiled meat.
❖ Stir frequently for 7 minutes.
❖ Pour 1 litre boiled water and stock from meat, then add washed rice.
❖ Boil slowly for 10 minutes and add mixed vegetables.
❖ Stir and add more boiled water if rice is not yet cooked.
❖ Continue to cook slowly until rice is properly cooked and

water dries up (rice should be moist, not watery).
- ❖ Garnish on plate with chopped parsley.
- ❖ Serve hot.

Serves 4

If you do not prefer your meat not well done, parboil meat instead of cooking till its tender before adding to saucepan with tomatoes and onion.

Beef, chicken, or pork can be used instead of lamb.

Epkwang (Cocoyams)

Ingredients:

3 large cocoyams
1 dried fish
250 g lamb pieces
100 g crayfish (ground)
250 g boneless peppered mackerel or any smoked boneless fish
1 medium onion
1 fresh chilli pepper or chilli sauce
1 litre boiled water
¼ litre palm oil
250 g fresh spinach leaves (a small bunch of spinach leaves) or
cocoyam leaves

Method:

❖ Peel, wash, and grate cocoyams.
❖ Mix grated cocoyams with water (60 ml) and a pinch of salt.
❖ Wash spinach leaves, or if in a bunch, take out leaves carefully and then wash.
❖ Put small amounts of grated cocoyam paste on the spinach or cocoyam leaves and roll into finger-like shapes.
❖ Arrange the rolled paste clockwise in a saucepan, leaving a hole in the centre.
❖ Pour half the boiled water in the centre of the saucepan and stand on low heat.
❖ Add the pieces of lamb and fish, palm oil, onion, fresh pepper or chilli sauce, **except crayfish**.
❖ Leave to boil for 10 minutes, and pour the rest of the boiled

water into the hole in the middle and **do not stir**.

❖ Add salt to taste and crayfish and simmer for 40 to 60 minutes.

❖ Stir and serve hot.

Serves 4

Sunday Roast Chicken with Garlic Stew

Ingredients:

1 whole chicken
1 large onion
1 can chopped tomatoes or 3 fresh tomatoes
3 cloves garlic (grated)
1 tsp pureed ginger
1 fresh chilli pepper (optional)
1 tsp chopped thyme
1 tsp chopped basil
¼ litre cooking oil
salt to taste
2 cubes Maggi

Method:

❖ Stuff chicken with of all ingredients, except tomatoes and cooking oil.
❖ Leave chicken for 30 minutes to allow seasoning to penetrate, then roast in a greased roasting tray for 45 minutes at Gas 4 (180°C or 350°F)
❖ Meanwhile, stir-fry onion in hot oil in a saucepan until golden brown, and add tomatoes, the rest of the ingredients, and garlic.
❖ Simmer and stir for 15 to 20 minutes
❖ Add steamed mixed vegetables and serve sauce with the **roasted chicken** and **rice** or ***Sauteed Yams.***

Beef or lamb can also be used in place of chicken.

Coconut Curried Lamb

Ingredients:

2 lb lamb cut into small pieces (1½ inch chunks)
5 tbs curry powder
2 cloves garlic (grated)
1 tbs chopped thyme
125 ml water
500 ml coconut milk
2 small onion (chopped)
1 chilli pepper
1 tbs chives (chopped)
2 Maggi cubes
salt to taste
4 tbs cooking oil

Method:

❖ Marinate lamb with one Maggi cube, thyme, garlic, and chives.
❖ Stir onion in hot cooking oil in medium sized saucepan until golden brown.
❖ Add marinated lamb and stir-fry on low heat until lamb is cooked and golden brown.
❖ Mix curry powder with the water and add to saucepan.
❖ Add the rest of the ingredients **except coconut milk,** and simmer for 5 minutes.
❖ Add coconut milk and simmer for 10 to 15 minutes.
❖ Serve with hot rice or *Spiced Mashed & Moulded Cassava.*

Serves 4 to 6

Beef Stew

Ingredients:

500 g beef pieces
2 tbs vegetable oil
2 onions (chopped)
1 can chopped tomatoes (crushed in a food blender)
2 garlic cloves (minced)
2 tbs chopped thyme
2 tbs chopped chives
2 cubes Maggi
1 tbs ground black pepper
1 fresh chilli pepper (optional)

Method:

❖ Boil beef together with the following ingredients: onion, Maggi, black pepper, garlic, chilli pepper, and salt to taste.
❖ Heat oil in a large saucepan and add the rest of onions. Stir until golden brown, add garlic and chilli peppers, and saute for 3 minutes.
❖ Then add tomatoes, Maggi cube, chives, thyme, and black pepper.
❖ Simmer for 30 minutes.
❖ Pour in the cooked beef together with stock and simmer for 30 minutes.
❖ Add a little water if necessary to prevent sticking, and salt to taste.
❖ Simmer for 5 minutes and serve hot with **Boiled Yams** or rice.

Ndole (Bitter Leaves Soup)

Ingredients:

2 lb fresh or dried bitter leaves
2 lb beef and smoked fish
2 fresh tomatoes (chopped)
1 medium sized onion
2 lb peanuts
1 tbs each pureed garlic and ginger (optional)
2 tbs cooking oil
3 Maggi or Knorr beef cubes
100 g crayfish (ground)
salt and pepper to taste

Method:

❖ Soak *dried bitter leaves* in water for at least 6 hours or overnight, and then boil for 15 minutes.
❖ Wash and squeeze out excess water.
❖ For *fresh bitter leaves*, chop and boil for 15 minutes, wash thoroughly, and squeeze excess moisture.
❖ Meanwhile, boil beef with onion, salt and pepper, and 1 cube.
❖ Boil peanuts for 10 minutes, peel off skin, and blend with 250 ml of water.
❖ Heat oil in a large saucepan, add chopped onions and tomatoes, stir and cook for 7 to 10 minutes.
❖ Add blended peanuts, beef and stock, smoked fish, cubes, ginger, and garlic and cook on low heat for 10 minutes.
❖ Add bitter leaves and simmer for 5 to 7 minutes.

❖ Add crayfish and simmer for another 5 minutes.
❖ Stir and serve with **_Boiled Plantains_** or **_Yams_**.

Please note this vegetable is rare (found mainly in Cameroon), therefore spinach can be used as a substitute.

Coconut Chicken with Lemongrass

Ingredients:

1 kg chicken drumsticks
2 tbs minced chives
2 cloves minced garlic
1 chopped onion
1 tbs vegetable oil
1 yellow chopped chilli pepper
2 stalks fresh lemongrass finely sliced
125 ml coconut milk
½ lime
salt and black pepper

Method:

❖ Season drumsticks with chives, salt, and black pepper for 10 minutes.
❖ Stir-fry chicken in garlic, chilli pepper, and lemongrass for 2 minutes.
❖ Add tomatoes and coconut milk, and simmer for 10 minutes.
❖ Take out drumsticks, leave sauce to cool, and then puree sauce in a blender and return sauce to pan (optional).
❖ Add drumsticks and cook for 5 minutes,
❖ Sprinkle lime juice and serve with rice, **Boiled Yams**, or **Plantains**.

Meat Loaf:

Ingredients:

500 g minced beef
1 onion (chopped)
1 tbs chopped parsley
salt to taste
1 tsp hot pepper sauce (optional)
1 egg
2 tbs breadcrumbs

Method:

❖ Preheat oven to gas 6 (200°C or 400°F).
❖ Mix beef, onion, parsley, salt, pepper, and breadcrumbs together.
❖ Add whisked egg and bind mixture together.
❖ Put mixture in a greased bread tin or any baking tin, and bake for 50 minutes or until cooked.
❖ Turn the loaf on a serving dish.
❖ Serve with **Sauté Cassava**, potatoes, and steamed vegetables.

Achu Soup

A really traditional dish, which is a favourite
of my land of origin—Bambili/Mbatu.

Ingredients:

2 tbs complete Achu spices
1 small piece of kanwa
80 ml palm oil (warmed up, not heated)
salt to taste
2 Maggi cubes
1 kg beef pieces (boiled with 1 chilli pepper, yellow preferably
for flavour)

Method:

❖ Dissolve kanwa in warm water.
❖ Pour in palm oil, stirring continuously as you pour, until
mixture turns yellow.
❖ Add boiled beef with stock left to cool.
❖ Add salt, Maggi cubes, and complete Achu spices to taste.
❖ Serve on its own in a bowl, or with pounded cocoyams on a
plate with a well in the middle, also known as Achu and eaten
with fingers.

Sometimes a little bit of the pounded coco yams is used in the
soup as a thickener.

Vegetarian Dishes

Red Kidney Beans Stew

Ingredients:

2 cans boiled kidney beans or 200 g unboiled
1 medium sized onion (chopped)
2 fresh tomatoes (medium)
1 chilli pepper
1/3 litre cooking oil
2 Maggi cubes
3 basil leaves
50 g crayfish
salt to taste

Method:

❖ Open the cans, pour contents in a colander, rinse out the reddish water, and leave to drain. Or boil beans until tender and rinse out boiled water.
❖ Blend tomatoes and chilli pepper in a wet blender.
❖ Heat the oil in a saucepan and fry the onion until golden brown, and then add the tomatoes with pepper, Maggi cubes, basil, and salt to taste.
❖ Simmer for 25 minutes until the consistency is thick and well blended.
❖ Add ground crayfish and simmer for 5 minutes.
❖ Serve with steamed carrots, peas, green beans and ***Boiled Ripe Plantains***, rice or ***Puff Puff***.

Corn Chave

This dish is prepared in exactly the same way as ***Red Kidney Bean Stew,*** except that sweet corn is added to the stew and simmered.

Okra Soup

Ingredients:

400 g sliced okra
200 g egusi (ground)
1 small fresh chilli pepper
all purpose seasoning (Dunn River)
1 small onion (chopped)
salt to taste

Method:

❖ Heat oil in a saucepan and fry onion until golden brown.
❖ Mix egusi with warm water to form a paste and pour into the saucepan.
❖ Add seasoning and salt and stir frequently for 7 minutes.
❖ Blend okra together with fresh pepper in a wet blender, add to saucepan, and whisk with a wooden spoon.
❖ Add 250 ml water and simmer for another 7 minutes.
❖ Serve with **Fufu** or **Gari** (see *Core Dishes*).

A favourite of my children.

Soya Beans Sauce

Ingredients:

2 fresh tomatoes
200 g soya beans
1 medium sized onion
1 tbs thyme
1 vegetable cube (Knorr)
salt to taste
1 chilli pepper (optional)
parsley for garnishing

Method:

❖ Roast soya beans till brown in colour.
❖ Peel off skin and grind to powder form.
❖ Fry the chopped onions and tomatoes together on low heat in a saucepan for 10 minutes.
❖ Add seasoning, thyme, salt, vegetable cube, pepper, and soya powder and cook until a nice thick sauce is obtained.
❖ Serve with boiled rice or **Green Rice** (see *Core Dishes*).

Fish or meat can also be used in this dish.

Coconut Rice

Ingredients:

1 tbs vegetable oil
1 medium sized onion (chopped)
300 g rice (parboiled)
150 ml coconut milk
2 vegetable cubes
1 tsp salt
3 fresh tomatoes
¾-1 litre water
25 g chopped chives

Method:

❖ Heat oil in a saucepan and add onion and tomatoes.
❖ Stir frequently until tomatoes are cooked.
❖ Add water, coconut milk, vegetable cubes, salt, and rice, and cook for 5 minutes, then reduce heat and simmer until rice is ready.
❖ Sprinkle with chives and serve hot with **Steamed Green Beans**.

Koki Beans:

Ingredients:

200 g peeled black-eyed beans
½ litre palm oil
1 litre water
a handful of sliced fresh spinach or cocoyam leaves
salt and Maggi cubes to taste
foil paper or warmed plantain leaves to wrap food
1 finely chopped onion
2 fresh yellow chilli peppers (optional)

Method:

❖ Soak black-eyed beans in water for 4 hours (at least).
❖ Heat oil in a saucepan until hot but not too hot.
❖ Rinse beans and blend in a wet blender or mortar together with chilli pepper.
❖ Mix beans with oil, salt, onion, and leaves. The mixture should be a dropping consistency.
❖ Scoop out small amounts into foil paper, then tie the top end to form a bundle.
❖ Simmer for 1 hour.
❖ Remove from foil and serve with boiled or *Sauté Cassava*, *Yams* or *Plantains*.

NB: To avoid spillage when pouring mixture onto foil paper, place foil paper on a round small bowl or colander to create the well for pouring the mixture.

Sauté Cassava

See core dishes. Serve with koki beans.

Baked Sweet Potato

Ingredients:

2 sweet potatoes (peeled and sliced into rectangular shapes, with ¼ inch thickness)
2 tbs brown sugar
1 tsp nutmeg
3 tbs vegetable oil
1 tbs lime juice

Method:

❖ Preheat oven to 180°C or 350°F.
❖ Grease a baking tray or bowl with vegetable oil.
❖ Mix the brown sugar with grated nutmeg.
❖ Place sweet potato slices side by side on the shallow baking dish or tray, then sprinkle the lime juice over and **lightly** cover potatoes with the brown sugar and nutmeg mixture.
❖ Bake for 10 to 12 minutes, then turn slices over and sprinkle with lime juice and brown sugar mixture again.
❖ Return to oven and bake for another 10 minutes.
Serve hot.

Serves 4

Fried Spinach

Ingredients:

2 bunches of spinach (chopped) or 1 kg chopped spinach
1 onion (sliced)
3 fresh tomatoes
¼ litre palm oil
80 ml water
3 Maggi cubes
salt to taste
1 fresh chilli pepper (puree)

Method:

❖ Crush tomatoes and pepper in a wet blender.
❖ Fry onion in hot palm oil in a frying pan.
❖ Add tomato and chilli mixture to frying pan and stir-fry until almost all of the water dries up.
❖ Squeeze out water from spinach, and stir in spinach.
❖ Add Maggi cubes and salt to taste.
❖ Stir-fry vegetables for 7 to 10 minutes and serve hot with **Fufu Corn** or any boiled *Core Dishes*.

Cassava Leaves

A Real Liberian Dish

Ingredients:

250 ml palm oil
1 medium onion
500 g cassava leaves (ground)
2 fresh small tomatoes
1 chilli pepper
2 bullion or Maggi cubes

Method:

❖ Bring palm oil to boil.
❖ Add ground cassava leaves, onion, tomatoes, pepper, and seasoning to taste.
❖ Add 125 ml water and boil for 15 to 20 minutes (more water can be added if preferred) or to a moist, rich consistency.
❖ Serve on a bed of rice.

Meat can also be used if desired.

Vegetable Stew

Ingredients:

400 g mixed vegetables (green beans, carrots, peas, broccoli, sweet corn)
2 tbs vegetable oil
2 onions (chopped)
1 can chopped tomatoes (crushed in a food blender)
2 garlic cloves (minced)
2 tbs chopped thyme
2 tbs chopped chives
2 cubes Maggi
1 tbs ground black pepper
1 fresh chilli pepper (optional)

Method:

❖ Steam vegetables with of the following ingredients: onion, Maggi, black pepper, garlic, chilli pepper, and salt to taste.
❖ Heat oil in a large saucepan and add the rest of onions, stir until golden brown, add garlic and chilli peppers, and sauté for 3 minutes.
❖ Then add tomatoes, Maggi cube, chives, thyme, and black pepper.
❖ Simmer for 30 minutes.
❖ Pour in steamed vegetables and simmer for 5 minutes.
❖ Add a small amount of water if necessary to prevent sticking.
❖ Add salt to taste, simmer for 5 minutes, and serve hot with **Boiled Yams** or rice.

Sautéed Green Beans in Garlic & Mild Chilli Sauce

Ingredients:

2 lb green beans
1 tbs vegetable oil
2 cloves garlic (puree)
mild chilli sauce
salt to taste
1 tbs ground black pepper

Method:

❖ Cut green beans to 2 inch slices and wash.
❖ Heat oil in a sauté pan and add garlic puree. Sauté till fragrant.
❖ Add green beans, salt, black pepper, and mild chilli sauce, and stir.
❖ Sauté for 10 minutes or until beans are tender.
❖ Serve on its own, or with a meat or fish dish.

Core Dishes

🍴🍽️🔪

Fufu Corn

Ingredients:

A small packet or 400 g of corn or maize flour
½ litre boiled water
½ litre warm water
cling film

Method:

❖ Mix corn flour with warm water to form a paste.
❖ Pour paste into a saucepan and stir briskly on medium heat.
❖ When hardened, add boiled water and stir continuously.
❖ Cover and simmer on very low heat for 10 minutes.
❖ Then stir until mixture becomes stiff and smooth.
❖ Remove in small heaps and wrap each heap in cling film or warmed plantain leaves.
❖ Serve hot with **Okra Soup**. Remove from cling film when about to eat (see *Vegetarian Dishes* and glossary page for **Okra Soup**).

Serves 4

Sometimes, the rough mixture called *kende* is cooked before adding the corn flour mixture.

Green Rice

Ingredients:

300 g rice
a handful of chopped spinach leaves or cress leaves
1 tbs butter or margarine
¾ litre water or enough to cook rice

Method:

❖ Put washed rice into a saucepan of boiling water and add salt.
❖ Cook rice until almost cooked then add washed vegetables seasoned with butter and simmer until ready.
❖ Serve hot with **West African Chicken Stew** or **Curry** (see *Meat Dishes*).

Serves 4

Plantain Chips (Dodo)

Ingredients:

2 ripe plantains
1 pinch or two of salt
cooking oil for frying

Method:

❖ Wash and peel plantains, and slice into long strips about 2 inches wide and 5 inches long or into long slanting slices.
❖ Cover ¼ of frying pan with oil and heat until hot.
❖ Add plantain slices seasoned with salt to fry.
❖ Fry until lightly brown on both sides.
❖ Remove and drain in a colander.
❖ Do not allow plantains to soak in oil.
❖ Serve with grilled or **Ginger Fish**.

Gari

Ingredients:

300 g gari
750 ml water

Method:

❖ Pour garri over boiling water, stirring continuously.
❖ Stir until well mixed and drain off excess.
❖ Make a firm but not too hard dough.
❖ Remove in small heaps and serve with **Okra Soup** (see *Vegetarian Dishes*).

Puff Puff

Ingredients:

200 g flour
¼ litre water
¼ litre milk
2 tbs margarine
2 eggs
50 g sugar
4 tsp baking powder
1 tsp salt
cooking oil to fry (vegetable or sunflower)
1 tsp nutmeg

Method:

❖ Rub margarine into flour until mixture is fine.
❖ Make a well in the middle of the bowl and add in sugar, milk, whisked eggs, and baking powder.
❖ Start mixing from the middle till all the flour is taken in. The mixture should be a soft dropping consistency.
❖ Leave in a warm place for mixture to rise.
❖ Deep fry small amounts until golden brown.
❖ Drain in a colander and serve with **Red Kidney Bean Stew,** or on its own as a snack.

Sauté Cassava:

Ingredients:

500 g cassava, peeled and sliced in to 4 inch pieces (squares)
2 small onions (sliced)
½ chilli pepper (chopped)
2 garlic cloves (grated)
2 tbs thyme
25 g chopped celery
25 g chopped parsley
a sprinkle of black pepper

Method:

❖ Peel, slice, remove the centre fibre, and boil cassava (adding a pinch of salt) until tender for about 25 minutes, then drain and cool.
❖ Fry onions, peppers, and garlic in a nonstick pan of hot oil for 5 minutes, then add cassava, celery, thyme, and season with salt and black pepper.
❖ Stir-fry carefully until cassava is golden.
❖ Serve hot with ***Fried Spinach***.

Roasted Yams

Ingredients:

2 lb yams
¾ litre water (to parboil yams)
60 ml vegetable oil

Method:

❖ Preheat oven to 200°C or 400°F (Gas 6).
❖ Grease a roasting tray and place parboiled yams.
❖ Bake yams for 20 minutes on each side, placing tray near the top of the oven.
❖ Serve with **Fish Stew**, **Vegetable Stew** or with **Fried Spinach**.

Boiled Yams

Ingredients:

1 kg yams
Water enough to simmer
A pinch of salt

Method:

❖ Wash, slice, and peel yams.
❖ Wash yams again and simmer with just enough amount of water.
❖ Add the salt and cook until soft.

To test if yam is ready, use a fork and prick through yams. If it splits easy, then it is ready. NB: Do not overcook yams.

How to peel yams:

❖ It is always easier to slice yams in to several slices before peeling.
❖ Peel by running the knife counterclockwise through sliced pieces.
❖ Or use a potato peeler and scrape out peelings.

Cassava Fufu

Ingredients:

500 g cassava flour
2 litres water
foil paper or plantain leaves

Method:

❖ Bring to boil ¾ of water in a large nonstick saucepan and mix cassava flour with the rest of the cold water.
❖ Pour into the saucepan of hot water the cassava mixture, stirring continuously until it blends.
❖ Cover and simmer for 10 minutes.
❖ Open the lid and sprinkle the rest of the flour and stir vigorously.
❖ When the colour has almost changed from white to opaque, cover again for 3 minutes.
❖ Stir and scoop out in small heaps and tie in the foil paper.
❖ Unwrap and serve hot with **Eru** or **Okra Soup**.

Boiled Green & Ripe Plantains

Boiled Green Plantains

Ingredients:

3 plantain fingers
750 ml water
a pinch of salt

Method:

❖ Peel plantains by trimming the edges, then running the tip of the knife straight down the plantain, making a small slit.
❖ Peel off green skin completely and brush knife over plantain to produce a smooth surface.
❖ Cut each plantain into two halves, and wash and boil with a pinch of salt.
❖ Cook for 20 minutes and serve with **Fried Spinach, Beef Curry** or **Groundnut Sauce with Beef**.

Boiled Ripe Plantains

Ingredients:

3 plantain fingers
750 ml water
a pinch of salt

Method:

❖ Peel plantains, firstly by trimming both ends (edges), then running the tip of the knife straight down the plantain, making a small slit.

❖ Peel yellow skin off completely.

❖ Cut each plantain into two halves, and wash and boil with a pinch of salt.

❖ Cook for 15 to 20 minutes and serve with **Spicy Coconut Fish with Lemon Grass** or **Koki Beans**.

Boiled Cassava

Ingredients:

3 medium cassavas
water to boil (about 700 ml)
a pinch of salt

Method:

❖ Peel cassavas and boil with salt until soft (15 to 20 minutes).

How to peel cassavas:

❖ Run the tip of the knife straight down the cassava, making a small slit.
❖ Then peel away both the brown rough skin and the pink skin from the cassava.
❖ Cut open cassava and remove the hard inner fibre.
❖ Cassava is now ready to be sliced, washed, and boiled.

Spiced Mashed and Moulded Cassava

Ingredients:

3 cassavas
a small bundle of fresh leeks (chopped)
1 small onion
salt to taste
1 tsp chopped thyme, basil, and chives
1 Maggi cube (crushed)

Method:

- ❖ Peel and slice cassava to small sizes.
- ❖ Wash slices and cook till tender enough to be mashed.
- ❖ Mix cassava with leeks, onions, herbs, and salt.
- ❖ Mould into preferred sizes.
- ❖ Serve with **Chicken Curry** or **Coconut Curried Lamb**.

Chilli Sauce

Ingredients:

3 chilli pepper
2 garlic cloves
300 ml cooking oil
a pinch salt
1 fresh tomato
1 tsp all purpose seasoning
1 small onion (chopped finely)

Method:

- ❖ Blend chilli peppers, garlic and tomatoes.
- ❖ Chop onions finely and fry in a saucepan.
- ❖ Add blended mixture to the saucepan.
- ❖ Simmer for 10 to 15 minutes, adding salt to taste.
- ❖ Serve with most savoury dishes.

Yams Sauté

Ingredients:

500 g yams, peeled and sliced into 4 inch pieces (squares)
2 small onions (sliced)
½ chilli pepper (chopped)
2 garlic cloves (grated)
2 tbs thyme
25 g chopped celery
25 g chopped parsley
a sprinkle of black pepper

Method:

❖ Slice, peel, and boil yams (adding a pinch of salt) until tender for about 15 minutes, then drain and cool.
❖ Fry onions, peppers, and garlic into a nonstick pan of hot oil for 5 minutes, then add yams, celery, thyme, and season with salt and black pepper.
❖ Stir-fry carefully until yams are golden. Add seasoning to taste.
❖ Serve hot with **Fried Spinach** (see *Vegetarian Dishes*).

Fish Dishes

Creole Fish Fillets

Ingredients:

1 tbs chives (minced)
2 tbs thyme (minced)
2 cloves grated garlic
1 kg firm fish fillets (salmon, haddock, or kingfish)
2 tbs olive oil
1 small onion (chopped)
2 chopped fresh tomatoes
hot chilli pepper
salt and coarsely ground black pepper

Method:

❖ Marinade fillets with thyme, garlic, chives, salt, and black pepper (to taste) for an hour.
❖ Sauté onions, chilli pepper, and tomatoes in a saucepan for about 12 minutes with hot olive oil.
❖ Add very little water (50 ml) and simmer for 5 minutes.
❖ Add in fish fillets to soak in sauce. Cook for 3 to 5 minutes on each side.
❖ Serve with **Roasted Plantains, Dodo** or **Baked Yams** (see *Core Dishes*).

Serves 4

Shrimp Curry

Cook in exactly the same way as West African Chicken Curry, except that shrimp are used instead of chicken.

Marinate shrimp in minced garlic, chilli pepper, and coarse black pepper before using.

Steamed Croker Fish with Njangsang

Ingredients:

2 medium sized croker or any white fish fillet
300 g njansang
250 g plantain flour (optional)
1 hot pepper or 200 g black pepper
salt to taste
2 Maggi cubes
foil paper (suitable for fish to fit)

Method:

❖ Blend njangsang until smooth.
❖ Add salt and plantain flour to blended njangsang and mix with water to make a paste.
❖ Remove bones from fish and coat fish with the paste and season with salt and pepper.
❖ Place the coated fish on to the foil paper and tie the top end to form a bundle.
❖ Place bundle into a pot with boiling water (enough to simmer).
❖ Simmer for 40 to 45 minutes and serve.

NB: To avoid spillage when pouring mixture onto foil paper, place foil paper on a round small bowl or colander to create the well for pouring the mixture.

Roasted Fish

Ingredients:

1 large fish (boneless or with bones)
1 onion (chopped)
2 Maggi cubes
2 tbs fish seasoning (Dunn River)
1 tbs minced ginger
1 tbs minced garlic
Salt to taste
½ lime

Method:

❖ Clean and wash fish, taking out gills, fins, and scales.
❖ Squeeze the lime on to the fish, leave for 2 minutes, then rinse the fish and dry with a cloth.
❖ Season fish with ingredients and leave for 20 minutes.
❖ Grill on either side and serve hot with **Dodo** and **Chilli Sauce.**
❖ If you have used a fish with bones, watch out for bones.

Serves 4

Spicy Coconut Fish with Lemongrass

Ingredients:

6 fish steaks (herring, carite, salmon, etc.)
2 tbs minced chives
2 cloves minced garlic
1 chopped onion
1 tbs vegetable oil
1 yellow chopped chilli pepper
2 stalks fresh lemongrass finely sliced
125 ml coconut milk
½ small lemon
Salt and black pepper

Method:

❖ Season steaks with chives, salt, and black pepper for 10 minutes.
❖ Stir-fry garlic, chilli pepper, and lemongrass in hot oil for 1 minute.
❖ Add tomatoes and coconut milk, and simmer for 10 minutes.
❖ Leave sauce to cool, and then puree sauce in a blender and return sauce to pan.
❖ Add fish steaks and cook for 5 minutes on either side.
❖ Sprinkle lemon juice and serve with rice, **Boiled Yams**, *Plantains*.

Ginger Fish or Fried Fish

Ingredients:

8 fish steaks (herring, haddock, mackerel, carite)
1 onion (chopped)
1 tbs chilli powder
2 tbs minced fresh ginger
3 tbs cooking oil (sunflower, corn, or vegetable oil)
salt to taste
2 Maggi cubes

Method:

❖ Marinate fish with ginger, onion, chilli pepper, salt, and crushed Maggi in a deep bowl. Leave to stand for 10 to 15 minutes.
❖ Fry fish in hot oil on either side until brown.
❖ Remove and drain in a colander.
❖ Serve with Rice and *Vegetable Stew*.

Fried Spinach with Fish

Prepare same as *Fried Spinach (Vegetarian Dishes)*, except add steamed peppered mackerel or any other steamed fish. Also add ground crayfish and stir-fry for 3 minutes. Serve with *Fufu Corn* are any *Boiled Core Dish*.

Egusi, Fish and Rice Koki

Ingredients:

100 g ground egusi
100 g parboiled rice
100 g crayfish
¼ kg smoked fish (use any flaky white fish, e.g. haddock, tuna, carite)
1 Maggi cube
1 small onion (chopped)
salt and black pepper to taste
1 tbs chilli sauce (optional)
50 ml cooking oil

Method:

❖ Mix ground egusi with warm water to form a dropping consistency.
❖ Mix egusi with parboiled rice until well blended.
❖ Add fish, crayfish, salt and pepper and mix together.
❖ Pour small amounts unto greased double folded foil paper, sealing the top end of the foil after pouring in the mixture.
❖ Steam cook for 1 hour.
❖ Serve hot.

NB: To avoid spillage when pouring mixture onto foil paper, place foil paper on a round small bowl, to create the well for pouring the mixture.

Mboh or Groundnut Koki:

Ingredients:

300 g groundnut (smooth paste)
100 g flaky white fish (salmon, tuna, mackerel)
1 medium onion
salt and chilli pepper to taste
foil paper

Method:

❖ Grind roasted groundnut in a dry blender to a smooth paste.
❖ Steam fish with chopped onion, salt, and pepper.
❖ Mix groundnut with steamed fish mixture.
❖ Pour small amounts onto greased double folded foil paper, sealing the top end of the foil after pouring in the mixture.
❖ Steam cook for 20 minutes.
❖ Serve with bread or **Boiled Green Plantains.**

Okra Soup

Prepare the same as in *Vegetarian Dishes*, except use a steamed or smoked fish, e.g. peppered mackerel, herring, croker, cod, plaice, crayfish, etc.

Fish and Tomato Casserole

Ingredients:

500 g white fish fillet
1 tbs chopped parsley
25 g margarine or butter
25 g breadcrumbs
salt and black pepper or hot pepper sauce
50 g cheese
1 small onion (sliced)
2 fresh tomatoes (chopped)

Method:

❖ Melt butter in a saucepan and add onions and tomatoes.
❖ Simmer for 5 minutes and add salt, pepper, and parsley.
❖ Add grated cheese and bread crumbs.
❖ Pour mixture over fish in a greased casserole dish.
❖ Bake for 30 minutes at gas 4 (180°C or 350°F).
❖ Serve with steamed carrots and **Sauté Cassava**.

Eru

Ingredients:

400 g eru leaves
1 kg spinach leaves (chopped leaves)
1 kg any smoked fish or peppered mackerel
¼ palm oil
1 hot pepper (optional)
2 Maggi cubes
200 g crayfish
salt to taste
¼ litre water

Method:

❖ Simmer spinach leaves for 10 minutes, add eru leaves, and stir to blend vegetables.
❖ Add salt, Maggi cubes, water, and ground hot pepper, and bring to boil for 10 minutes.
❖ Add palm oil and fish, and simmer.
❖ Lastly, mix in crayfish.
❖ Leave for 5 minutes and stir.
❖ Serve hot with **Cassava Fufu.**

Can also be used as a meat dish, in which case, meat is used instead of fish or together with fish.
Frozen chopped spinach leaves can be used as long as they are defrosted before weighing.
Cocoyam leaves can also be used instead of spinach leaves.

Sese Cocoyams with Fish

Ingredients:

5 large cocoyams
1 large onion
½ kg peppered mackerel (boneless)
3 Maggi cubes
a handful of chopped fresh spinach leaves or frozen spinach
¼ litre palm oil
2 medium sized fresh tomatoes
200 g crayfish
750 ml water or water above level of cocoyams
1 fresh hot pepper
salt and ground black pepper to taste

Method:

❖ Peel and wash cocoyams. Slice into 3-inch chunks.
❖ Bring cocoyams to boil and add all ingredients except crayfish and mackerel.
❖ Cook cocoyams for 20 minutes then add crayfish and mackerel.
❖ Simmer for 15 minutes to get a rich consistency. By this time the palm oil should have penetrated the cocoyams.
❖ Serve hot.

Fish Stew

Ingredients:

1 kg fish steaks (beam, croaker, mackerel)
1 large onion
1 can chopped tomatoes
1 chilli pepper (optional)
2 peppers
1 tsp ground coriander
2 cloves minced garlic
1 tsp minced ginger
1 tsp freshly ground black pepper
1 tsp fresh thyme
salt and Maggi cubes to taste
200 g mixed vegetables (carrots, peas, green beans, sweet corn)

Method:

❖ Use fish steaks, or if whole, clean, wash, and slice into steaks.
❖ Season fish with half the amounts of garlic, ginger, onion, black pepper, chilli pepper (if using), salt, and Maggi cubes.
❖ Grill fish for 15 to 20 minutes.
❖ Meanwhile, fry onion and tomatoes in hot oil.
❖ Then add the rest of ingredients except mixed vegetables and cook for 20 minutes; add a little water if needed.
❖ Add mixed vegetables and simmer for 5 minutes.
❖ Add grilled fish and simmer for 2 minutes.

Serve with **Boiled Yams**, **Green Rice**, or **Plantains**.

Serves 4

Peanut Butter Sauce with Fish Steaks & Rice

Ingredient:

400 g roasted groundnut
1 kg fish Steaks
1 tsp freshly ground ginger and garlic each
1 can chopped tomatoes
1 medium onion
3 tbs groundnut oil
1/8 tsp turmeric
3 Maggi cubes
salt and fresh chilli to taste.

Method:

❖ Simmer fish steaks with salt, some slices of onion, and 1 Maggi cube.
❖ Heat oil in a saucepan and add the rest of onion and stir until golden brown
❖ Add tomatoes, garlic, and ginger.
❖ Cook sauce on very low heat until there is very little of the sour taste from tomatoes left.
❖ Crush groundnut in dry food processor and set aside, then add ¾ litre water to groundnut paste and mix well until smooth. Add to saucepan.
❖ Add fish steaks, Maggi cubes, salt, and chilli to taste.
❖ Simmer for 10 minutes.
❖ Serve hot with Rice or **Boiled Ripe Plantains.**

Serves 6

Chicken or beef can also be used in place of fish for this recipe.

Spicy Prawn Coconut with Lemongrass & Rice

Ingredients:

500 g large prawns (peeled)
2 tbs minced chives
2 cloves minced garlic
1 chopped onion
1 tbs vegetable oil
1 yellow chopped chilli pepper
2 stalks fresh lemongrass finely sliced
125 ml coconut milk
½ small lemon
salt and black pepper

Method:

❖ Season prawns with chives, salt, and black pepper for 10 minutes.
❖ Stir-fry garlic, chilli pepper, lemongrass in hot oil for 1 minute.
❖ Add tomatoes and coconut milk and simmer for 10 minutes.
❖ Leave sauce to cool, and then puree sauce in a blender and return sauce to pan.
❖ Add prawns and cook for 5 minutes on either side.
❖ Sprinkle lemon juice and serve with rice, **Boiled Yams**, *Plantains*.

Snacks &

Desserts

Sweet Potato Biscuits

Ingredients:

250 g flour
25 g mashed cooked sweet potatoes
25 g sugar
½ tsp salt
125 g margarine
150 ml milk to mix
2 tsp baking powder

Method:

❖ Sieve flour in a bowl and add all dry ingredients.
❖ Melt the fat in a saucepan and beat well into the mashed sweet potatoes. Stir in milk and beat thoroughly.
❖ Add the dry ingredients to the potato mixture and stir until well blended. Add a little more milk, if necessary, to make a soft but not wet dough.
❖ Turn onto a floured board or surface and roll out lightly, 1 cm thick.
❖ Prick and cut with a biscuit cutter and arrange on a greased baking tray.
❖ Bake in a moderately hot oven for 15 minutes. Gas 4 (180°C or 350°F).

Groundnut Macaroons

Ingredients:

100 g crushed peanuts
2 egg whites
120 g sugar

Method:

❖ Whisk egg whites and sugar into a saucepan of hot water until mixture is thick and fluffy.
❖ Lightly fold in the crushed peanuts until mixture is smooth.
❖ Drop spoonfuls on a greased baking tray. To decorate, on each macaroon place half a peanut before baking.
❖ Bake in a very slow oven. Gas 1 (140°C or 275°F) for 30 minutes.
❖ Macaroons harden as they cool.

Grated coconut can be used, but must be baked longer—for 45 minutes at the same temperature.

Exotic Fruit Pudding

Ingredients:

6 guavas
3 tbs honey
2 tbs sugar
breadcrumbs
Grated rind and juice of 1 lime

Method:

❖ Wash, peel, and slice fruit thinly.
❖ Grease a pie dish. Pack tightly with alternate layers of fruit and breadcrumbs, starting with breadcrumbs.
❖ Heat honey, sugar, water, and lime juice in a saucepan. Add rind of lime and stir. Pour mixture over fruit and breadcrumbs in pie dish.
❖ Bake in moderate heat. Gas 4 (180°C or 350°F) for an hour and a half.
❖ Serve hot with custard sauce.

Mangos and pawpaw may be used instead.

Pineapple Crisp & Ice Cream

Ingredients:

1 medium pineapple
2 tsp lime juice
2 tbs brown sugar

The topping:

5 tbs butter
150 g flour
4 tbs sugar
2 tbs brown sugar

Method:

❖ Preheat oven to 180°C
❖ Peel pineapple, trimming top and bottom, then cut open and remove inner core, and cut fruit into 2-inch length chunks.
❖ Mix lime juice, pineapple, and brown sugar together and place in a greased oven dish.
❖ For the topping, mix butter and flour together until mixture looks like crumbs, then add sugar and mix with hands.
❖ Place the mixture on to the pineapple, making sure all the fruit is covered, and finally, sprinkle with brown sugar.
❖ Bake for 40 minutes or until crisp.
❖ Serve with ice cream.

Lemon Biscuits

Ingredients:

100 g plain flour
50 g butter
50 g granulated sugar (plus a little extra to sprinkle on top)
1 egg
1 level tsp lemon rind

Method:

❖ Heat oven to gas mark 4 (180°C or 350°F).
❖ Separate the egg white from the yolk.
❖ Wash and grate lemon rind finely.
❖ Put flour and butter into a mixing bowl and rub together, then stir in sugar and rind.
❖ Add egg yolk and mix to a smooth dough.
❖ Knead lightly and roll out thinly. Cut into 15 biscuits with lemon shaped cutters or any of your choice.
❖ Place on a greased baking tray, brush with beaten egg white, and sprinkle with a little sugar.
❖ Bake for 12 to 15 minutes or until pale gold. Leave to cool on tray and serve.

Elephant Treat

Ingredients:

8 small pineapple chunks
a large scoop of coconut ice cream
one large black berry or red grape
2 thinly fried savoury pancakes
1 banana

Method:

❖ Place pineapple chunks into pancakes and make 2 triangular shapes.
❖ Place the triangularly shaped pancakes at horizontal ends of the plate.
❖ Carefully add a large scoop of coconut ice cream between the triangles.
❖ Cut the black berry into two halves and place each half at the top of the ice cream (to look like eyes).
❖ Peel a fresh looking banana and place with one end touching the ice cream and the other end pointing downwards (like an elephant's tusk).
❖ For best results, prepare and serve immediately.

Grilled Mangoes

Ingredients:

2 large mangoes, peeled and sliced into squares without the core
2 tsp lime juice
50 g brown sugar

Method:

❖ Place mango squares in foil and add sugar and lime juice.
❖ Wrap and grill for 12 to 15 minutes or until sugar has begun to caramelize.
❖ Remove from foil and place on a greased tin and grill directly until tender.
❖ Serve with ice cream.
❖ Pineapple may be used instead.

Pawpaw & Lime

Ingredients:

1 pawpaw
1 lime

Method:

❖ Cut pawpaw into four quarters and scoop out black seeds.
❖ Serve each half in a bowl with a slice of lime on top.
❖ Squeeze lime on to the pawpaw just before eating and *enjoy*.

Serves 4

Cameroon Bars

Ingredients:

150 g flour
50 g margarine
200 g brown sugar
3 eggs
2 tbs orange or lemon zest
1 tsp vanilla essence
2 tsp baking powder
a pinch of salt
75 g chopped groundnut (peanuts)
200 g chocolate pieces

Method:

❖ Line baking tray with foil paper or grease tin.
❖ Whisk together margarine, brown sugar, eggs, vanilla, lemon zest, and a pinch of salt till fluffy.
❖ Add flour and baking powder and fold well.
❖ Then fold in groundnuts and chocolate pieces.
❖ Spread mixture on greased tin and bake for 35 to 40 minutes on Gas 4 (180°C or 350°F).
❖ Cool and cut into bars, using a cutter or sharp knife.

Chin-Chin

Ingredients:

250 g flour
100 g fat
2 eggs
Pinch of salt
100 g sugar
lemon zest
vanilla essence (flavouring)
½ litre groundnut oil for frying
250 ml fresh milk or evaporated milk mixed with water
1 tsp baking powder

Method:

❖ Sieve flour, salt, and baking powder together.
❖ Rub margarine in flour with fingers until mixture resembles fine breadcrumbs.
❖ Make a well in the middle and add beaten eggs, milk, sugar, and flavouring.
❖ Mix to a stiff rollable mixture.
❖ Flatten on floured board with a rolling pin to about 2-inch thickness and cut in strips.
❖ Cut into desired shapes and deep fry until golden brown.
❖ Serve with a drink.

Fruit Basket

Ingredients:

1 pineapple
3 red cherries or strawberries
1 shot of rum
1 mango
1 orange
1 passion fruit
100 g fruits of the forest
2 guavas

Method:

❖ Cut pineapple straight down the middle into two halves and scoop out the fruit, leaving the juice.
❖ Dice all fruits including some of the pineapple (taken out) and place alternating to give a good mix of fruit and colour.
❖ Squirt in the juice from the passion fruit.
❖ Lastly, add the rum just before serving.

Perfect for romantic couples to share.

Pawpaw (Papaya) Extravaganza

Ingredients:

1 pawpaw
5 red cherries or strawberries
1 shot of rum
1 mango
1 orange
1 passion fruit
100 g fruits of the forest
2 guavas

Method:

❖ Cut pawpaw straight down the middle into two halves and scoop out the fruit, leaving the juice.
❖ Dice all fruits including some of the pawpaw (taken out) and place alternating to give a good mix of fruit and colour.
❖ Squirt in the passion fruit juice.
❖ Add rum just before serving.

Some Useful Suggestions for Special Occasions

Two friends are coming to spend the weekend with you, one is a **VEGETARIAN**. Here is an example of a three-course meal you could prepare for all of you to enjoy:

First Course:

Mushroom Pepper Soup

Second Course:

Sauté Yams with Fried Spinach
Koki Beans With Boiled Ripe Plantains

Third Course:

Exotic Fruit Pudding.

Your parents or in-laws are coming to your house for **SUNDAY ROAST**. Here are some examples of what you could prepare:

First Course:

Meat Suya

Second Course:

Groundnut (Peanut) Sauce with Beef and Rice
Sunday Roast Chicken or Lamb Stew with Garlic and Boiled Yams

Third Course:

Grilled Mangoes

You are preparing a meal for a family with young **CHILDREN**. Some examples of dishes you could make:

First Course:

Banana & Tomato Salad

Second Course:

Jollof Rice
Okra Soup and Fufu Corn

Third Course:

Pineapple Crisp & Ice Cream
Lemon Biscuits

You are planning to impress your partner on **VALENTINE'S DAY** by preparing a romantic meal for the two of you:

First Course:

Dodo (Plantain Chips) with Spicy Prawn Tomato Sauce

Second Course:

Spicy Coconut Fish with Lemongrass
Baked Sweet Potatoes

Third Course:

Fruit Basket

You are planning a **WEDDING PARTY**, or **ANNIVERSARY PARTY**. Here are a few suggestions:

First Course:

Yam Fritters
Sweet Potato Starters
Meat Suya

Second Course:

Coconut Rice
Koki Beans and Plantains
Sautéed Green Beans in Garlic & Mild Chilli Sauce

Dessert:

Sweet Potato Biscuits
Chin-Chin
Exotic Fruit Pudding

Please note that this is only a guide. You can use any dish you prefer.

Glossary

A dictionary of some of the foods.

All of these foods can be found in tropical foods stores in countries around the world and some in continental supermarkets.

Avocado:

This is a pear shaped fruit with a green skin, but creamy yellow inside. Delicious in salads and starters. Soft when ready to eat.

Cassava:

A root vegetable shaped like a big carrot with a brown skin and white flesh. It is usually boiled and prepared as a vegetable, or processed into GARI or TAPIOCA, as it mostly known

Chilli Pepper:

This is an extremely hot pepper species. They are green, red, and yellow, or even orange in colour. Known to release endorphins in the body.

Coconut:

A white substance with a black coating that clings to the rough brown shell of the nut. It can be eaten once the rough brown shell is split open and the water is removed.

Cocoyam:

A root vegetable, also with a brown skin and white flesh. Looks like a mix between a cassava and a yam, but smaller than a yam.

Dunn River:

This is an all purpose seasoning, which can be used for most savoury dishes.

Egusi:

A seed from the pumpkin plant. It is a delicious thickener for sauces and vegetables.

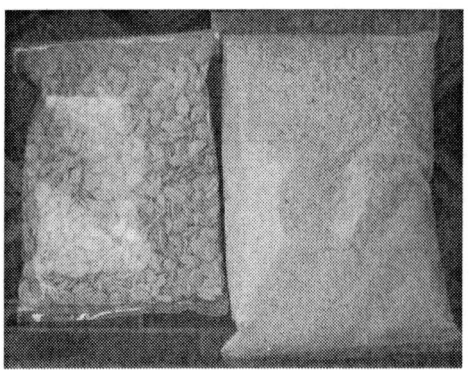

Fufu:

A white dough-like texture made from dried and ground maize. Also available in flour form for fast preparation.

Groundnut (peanut, monkey nut):

An underground bean with two kernels that grow in a pod/shell.

Maggi Cubes:

These are seasoning cubes, full of flavour and a great taste. They can be used for marinating meats, and to add taste to soups and vegetarian dishes.

Mango:

They can be succulent and juicy as well as hard in texture. Sweet tasting fruit—excellent as a drink and as a desert. Yellowish fruit inside once the skin has been peeled. The skin can be either greenish or yellowish.

Njangsang:

These are little brownish spices, similar in size, colour, and texture to sultanas. Once ground, they produce a powerful flavour; for use in soups.

Okra:

A great tasting vegetable, loved by both adults and kids. Can be cooked sliced or crushed in a wet blender. They are green with tiny spikes and with white tiny seeds inside.

Palm Oil:

A reddish yellow liquid produced from the oil palm fruit. It is very rich and oily and a good source of vitamin B.

Passion Fruit:

This is a fruit with a thick, non-edible outer peel, which cracks open revealing a juice with tiny black seeds. Quite sweet and sour in taste, with a high perfumed flavour.

Pawpaw (Papaya):

A green or yellowish fleshed fruit, filled with tiny black seeds in the centre. Skin turns from green to yellow when ready to eat.

Plantain:

A member of the banana family. Unlike bananas, plantains are not edible until cooked. They can be either green (figs) or yellow (ripe). The figs and ripe plantains can be boiled, fried, and roasted. As figs, they can be used in savoury dishes, and as ripe, used in desserts.

Pounded Yam:

A dough-like texture made from pounding boiled yams. Also
available in flour form for fast preparation.

Printed in the United Kingdom
by Lightning Source UK Ltd.
115194UKS00001B/16